Spy Pond

by Ed Meek

Ed Meek

Spy Pond

PROLIFIC PRESS

Acknowledgements

Some poems appearing in this collection previously appeared in these fine journals: *The Aurorean*: "Fog in Boston"; *Chest Magazine:* "Cough"; *The Christian Science Monitor*: "Field"; *Chronogram*: "In the Middle of Nowhere," "Silence"; *Cosmopsis Quarterly:* "Volcano Park"; *Dark Matter*: "Dark Matter"; *Lilies and Cannonballs Review*: "Pre-emptive Strikes"; *Loud Zoo:* "Death Panels"; *The Lyrical:* "Spy Pond," "Truth in Sentencing"; *Mobius*: "Powder Blue"; *Muddy River:* "The End of Summer"; *Muscle and Blood:* "At the Wake"; *The Prose Poem Project:* "Jessica"; *Plume:* "At the Lake"; *The Prompt:* "More or Less," "The Prompt," "Family Photo"; *Spillway:* "The Aroma of Pig"; *The Valley Review:* "Bone-house," "The Word Present"; *Wilderness House Literary Review:* "Gravity," "Negative Numbers," "Swimming."

ISBN-13: 978-1632750174 (Prolific Press)
ISBN-10: 1632750171
Published by Prolific Press Inc., Harborton, VA.
Edited by: Glenn Lyvers
Printed in the USA.

Contents

For Elizabeth

Inhabitants

If there is an Oversoul,
as the transcendentalists thought,
ghosts inhabit it...
Maybe Undersoul is more accurate.

Underneath the earth,
deep underground
a railroad, cars filled
with the dead children
of Sandy Hook, Columbine, Virginia Tech,
on their way to Paradise...

I like to think I hear the train whistle
in the distance as I walk to work,
and as I lie dreaming at night,
anxiously drifting in and out.

Drones

You can barely hear the dial-tone
that hums through the wires of your brain.
It is the call of drones, buzzing as they fly
on their secret missions
known only to those
who man the remote controls,
striking the keys to send
unmanned Hawks, Ravens and Shadows
deep into Pakistan.

We have absolute confidence
in our sources. Our President
is in command, making
the hard decisions. Later
he falls asleep to the monotone hum
in the back of his mind,
while Pakistanis, herding sheep,
look up, straining to hear
the unnerving buzz
of mechanical birds.

Downed Trees

It's unsettling to see a tree upended,
roots exposed like nerves
torn from the heart of the earth,
or the trunk of a 30 foot pitch pine
cracked in half—
you can almost hear
the aching series of splits,
the tree bending in high winds
      until the core splinters.
And the branches are strewn about,
like lost limbs that echo
Grendal's pathetic cries,
Boewulf's triumphant shouts.
We could use him now
to wrestle heat itself,
pin wind to the mat,
and subdue the seas.
We'll need heroic help
to change our fate.
Was it he who said,
"Fate often serves an undoomed man
if his courage is good"?
We could use some courage now
when trees snap like matchsticks in hurricane-winds
and the ocean, from whence we came,
seeks revenge for what we've done.

Spy Pond: Arlington, Massachusetts

*--In the 19th Century Spy Pond was a source
for ice cut into huge blocks...*

It's unnerving, when shuffling across the ice
in early March, to feel a shift beneath your feet
and hear the aching crack before you see
the crooked rift that cuts a seam between your legs.
You might have known it wasn't safe. You saw
the melting at the edge before you ventured out.
You know about the shifting seasons,
shorter winter, early spring, summer months
of record heat and drought. Just to be safe
you best drop down onto your hands and knees,
pray all the way to the shore.

Death Panels

She pokes the plastic tube
that snakes into her belly.
"What's this?" she asks.
"Feeding tube," I say.
She knows me
though she has forgotten
my name. I hold
her pale, limp hand.
"You have to feed yourself," I say,
but she has lost all interest
in food. She is already
halfway there, taken
to conversing with her dead
brothers and sisters. Meanwhile,
it's up to us to decide
when to say when.

We are her death panel,
my father, my sisters and I.
We must issue the orders
to her executioners,
the doctors, nurses, social workers.
Otherwise, they will play
Devil's advocate
and keep her alive
as long as they can.

Saffron

The pistils stand on end—thin red reeds
in a tiny glass bottle. When dropped
into boiling water with rice
they turn yellow and suffuse
the rice with sunlight
and the fragrance of lotus petals.

Who among us knows the origin of saffron?
The price in man-hours,
the tedious work of Mediterranean fingers.
Four thousand flowers for an ounce.
Seventy thousand stamens hand-picked
from the heart of the crocus make one pound.

Where does it all come from?
—the spices, the food, the shirt on your back?

The Aroma of Pig

Mornings, bacon revels in fat,
noisy with applause at its fate;
the depressed toaster jumps to its feet;
eggs happily join the party.

Why does it smell so good?
Cured ribbons of pig flesh. How
can we eat like this? Eggs
over easy, yellow stripes of yoke bleeding
from our mouths. Charcoal toast cupping butter
churned from the milk of cows.

How did this happen? Who was first
to follow in the awkward steps of the calf
to steal his mother's milk? Who decided
to run with the wolves and track
the scent of boar? Who first stripped
the wild pig, laced it with salt and cooked it
over a fire, sizzling in its own fat

while the rest of the clan awoke
smiling at the aroma
wafting in
the morning mist?

The Crow Knows

The crow knows all who follow
must obey the rhythm
of their own flight. Yet

the crow despises melody,
calls romance a song
for the hearing-impaired.

Crows tempt squirrels
across the road—
"Let's play chicken," they squawk.

The crow knows whom to trust.
He has friends in high places
and they all look like him.

Pre-emptive Strikes

One must imagine
"the worst" to be worse
than the worst imaginable.

Take a backdoor attack
with a dirty bomb,
envelopes stamped with anthrax,
cereal boxes sugared with smallpox.

There are knowns,
known unknowns,
and unknown unknowns.

The unknown unknowns,
Rumsfeld muses,
we don't even know
we don't know them.

Because anything is possible,
we must prevent it.

Powder Blue

Poet Richard Hugo once told me
he wanted a Mercedes—
powder blue. I scoffed,
then thought of his arthritic knees,
blackened lungs, dysfunctional liver—
30 years of cigarettes and booze.
He'd fought the last World War,
worked 15 years at Boeing.
He deserved a nice ride.
That was 30 years ago. Today
I bought a BMW,
titanium paint, xenon headlights,
moon roof, 17 inch
alloy wheels.

What did I do
to deserve this? Was I born
at the right time, here
in North America—
far from Al Qaeda's caves?
Don't I deserve to be scammed
by the venal salesman whose boss
pads the sticker with add-ons?
Wouldn't you like to vandalize my car,
gleaming in the driveway?

Say you were Arabic, pious
in your prayers to Allah,
your country run by
two-faced lackeys.
Wouldn't you love
to fly to America,
all expenses paid,
to place a plastic explosive
beneath the wheel of my car
and watch it blow
on the nightly news
me in it?

War Crimes

Lyndie England sits quietly
in her cell. She doesn't know
to this day what she did
wrong. She did what
she was told and ended up
here. Yes she played
the Raqs like dogs,
but hell, they are dogs,
and their book
which she tore up
and stuffed in their mouths
is nothing but gibberish
in Arab symbols. Lyndie knows
she's sitting here to pay
for the sins of civilians,
Rumsfeld and the Mexican—
Gonzalez, who, "don't know
what an order means."

Asymmetrical Warfare

"...and there are unknown unknowns."
(Donald Rumsfeld)

It's unnerving to think you might lose
your legs as you cross
the finish line of a marathon
after months of training
in the steel-eyed dawn
or in the stone-cold dark of winter,
riding the train out to Framingham weekends
to jog the route with others foolish or dedicated enough
to run 26.2 miles. It doesn't seem fair
that your family, there to cheer you on,
should be maimed where they stood
in the crowd at Copley Square.

*

And just how easy is it
to stuff a backpack
with shrapnel and fireworks
and set it off with a remote control?
—The manifestation of your radical beliefs—
true or false, we are the Great Satan,
not the Russians who bombed your Chechnya
but the U.S. who gave you asylum.

Our mistake to dangle the American Dream
of golden gloves and college degrees
while the sore wounds of Chechnya festered
and the salve of jihad called your name.

Art

Gustaf Miller stands behind the mini-skyscrapers
he created, constructions, he calls them.
From the ceiling hangs a plane
suspended in time. If it flew
into the tallest of the buildings,
it would knock it down
and Gustaf would set it right again.
He might have to re-hang the plane.

It would not cause a fire in the building
and freeze the elevators
and trap hundreds of people
above the 21st floor.
There are no people to jump out the windows.

There is no second plane,
no radical Muslims acting at the behest
of Osama Bin Laden, attacking
the Great Satan to die as martyrs.
There are no firefighters
to sacrifice their lives.

It is only art after all.
It can evoke memories
but cannot change
what happened. It can imitate
but cannot duplicate
life.

Bronze Crowd

--Sculpture
by Magdalena Abakanowicz

These figures stand their ground
defiant past the end.

Although they must feel something
has been lost and is now MIA—
blown away...

Are they thoughtless and carefree?
We may ask but they won't tell.
They remain mute
in the face of our questions.

Or do they still feel the wind
where their necks once were?
Their shoulders seem to smile.

Negative Numbers

are easy enough to understand
in the abstract.
They are on the opposite side
of the ledger,
underneath
positive numbers
that climb to heaven
like a ladder to the stars
while the negative numbers
plunge down
          seemingly endless steps

to the catacombs below.

Yet they balance the world of trade,
addition and multiplication
subtracted and divided.
We can't always see them
but we know they're there.

They represent loss,
what's gone, or missing, or stolen.
They operate in the shadow world
of debt, deficit and derivative.
We ignore them at our peril
because they can sneak up
behind us
          and jump on our back;
we may carry them for awhile;
eventually, they will weigh us down
and pin us to the ground
though we may crawl out from under them
on our hands and knees
one long day at a time.

Truth in Sentencing

Crystal Lynn, 22, was arrested
while walking on the bike path,
looking back over her shoulder.
She fit the description
of the girl who'd just hit
the East Cambridge Savings Bank
(white female, light hair, sweats).
She'd given the teller a note that read
>   Hand over cash
>   Or I'll set off a bomb
>   with my phone.

"I didn't do it! Another girl did!"
She told Somerville police
when they apprehended her,
and searching her person found
one hundred and ten twenty-dollar bills
stuffed in the pouch of her hoodie.
"Twenty of that is mine!" she said
as the officer cuffed her and ducked her
into the back seat of the cruiser.

Couldn't we start over?
Return the money to the bank.
Throw the note away.
Go back to bed.
Just say no.
Tell Junior hit the road.
Let him pimp someone else.
Let him pay his own way.

Whatever you do
don't drop out of school.
Stay in and do your work.
Don't hang out with him,
and fail to use protection.
Don't borrow his needle.
Don't get mom's boyfriend mad.
Don't tell mom

when he touches you.
What difference does it make?

What difference does it make now,
With your record
five years is a good deal
for armed robbery.

On Edge

Lizzie must have known it was high
enough before she jumped
from the 7th floor of her apartment in Paris.
Experts claim a psychotic break from reality occurs
suddenly sometimes, even in middle age.

Lizzie was about to turn 55, happily married,
we thought, with a cushy government job
and two successful daughters, both
beautiful and smart like her, and her
husband Pierre, a winner of the *Legion d'honneur*.

If you're psychotic, you can't tell
what's real and what is not,
like reality TV, or plastic surgery, or who
our enemy really is. You

enter the realm of doubt, darkness and depression—
dash out to the balcony and leap,
though leaping takes a kind of courage, a sort
of faith or lack thereof. You see
yourself at a dead end—
no way out
but down.

Yet Lizzie loved life! Sure, she loved to
drive fast, yet chose not to turn
            off the road
            over a cliff near her
gite in Corsica. Instead
she threw herself off the balcony as Pierre lay in bed, leaving us

to puzzle it out, put it into words, make sense of it,
to pull us back from the edge.

Calculated Risk

Dad down-shifts the Civic just before the intersection.
He thinks he's lucky the light is green.
His wife chatters about the graduation.
Their only daughter, the valedictorian,
sits behind mom, seatbelt snug. Dad
hears the sirens, catches the blue light
in the corner of his eye, the cruiser
coming on fast like a low flying jet.
He thinks, What? Hits the gas to get
out of the way, but the cruiser
hammers the Honda's rear passenger door,
crumpling the metal, fracturing the window,
the frame closing in on the daughter
like a metal claw, indifferent
to her screams, her flawless skin,
her taut muscles from years of dance,
her youth, her beautiful blue eyes.

She is lucky to survive, the doctors say.
Three months later she sits
in the wheelchair ready to go home.
She has full use of her left hand
and partial vision in her left eye.
She is optimistic about the future.

Dad blames himself for not seeing the cruiser sooner.
Mom blames the kid the cops were chasing,
the one who got away in the stolen car.
We all know there is no one to blame.

The Man of the Hand

You stand
off to the side
apart from the rest
but you are not lonely
or afraid to join in
and count to ten
or reassure
with a squeeze
or a clasp
and when required
help hold a pen.
You can close a deal
and grip like a claw
and if need be
lock knuckles
in a fist. You
are more than willing
to push a button
or approve
of something great
or work in opposition
and grasp a tool
you may have even
helped to fashion.
You are the man.

The Replacement

The clone is strangely lonely,
estranged even from himself.
He is like Albert Camus
times two. The clone feels guilty,
does he take up too much space?
Is he eating more than his fair share?
He too wants to be happy,
to live up to his Father's hopes and dreams.
He often wonders what's wrong
or right. He knows he is the same
yet different. Science is his Father,
his Mother, his God and Goddess.
And like the rest of us, he knows
he can be replaced.

Silence

"Silence is so accurate."
(Mark Rothko)

Silence is so inaccurate.
It is the sense of absence
when someone is gone.
It is the ellipsis at the end of the story...
It is not the comma, but the period.
It is the break at the end of the end-stopped line.

It fills the spaces between the fingers and toes.
It is the hesitation, the interior sigh,
the empty room after the door closes;

It is the blank page, the white space.
It is what remains unsaid.

Gravity

--14 pounds per square inch.

No wonder we're tired.
No wonder it's so hard
to get up out of bed.
That's why we sink into chairs
and fall asleep on couches.

It is the weight we carry
from birth to death.
It anchors us to the earth,
and we shrink from it.

Its song is the creak and groan in our bones
as we make our way home.

In the Middle of Nowhere

1.

This much you know,
for every positive number,
there's a negative
stretching to infinity
—in either direction—
and in-between,
cero, nol, nothing.
Of course there's a question
as to whether it really exists.
It's there because we put it there.
We like the idea
as long as it doesn't apply to us.
Anyway it's necessary.
If you take one away from one, what's left?
Look, you have to start somewhere.
This is what comes
before the beginning
and at the end: Ø

2.

Or maybe it's where
we come from and go to—
where we go through.
Nowhere we know
before we get there
or after we arrive.

Bone House

Body armor, birthday suit with mask,
elastic sock, prophylactic friend,
sometimes you balloon with fat,
other times you frame
muscle and bone. You bruise blue
and burn red and turn brown.
You blister, scab and peel and shed.
In your garden, hair grows
in clumps and patches, beards and staches,
curious brows. You pout
and sag and circle eyes in darkness.
You grow pale and sallow when sick.
You prick from pins
and pierce from needles,
cut with knives.
You wrinkle with age,
furrow, stretch and itch.
You are irreplaceable, implacable,
mined with pores, moist with sweat,
dried from years of sun.
You keep scars on display—
living memories, storylines
of battles won and lost.
And when the house falls
finally down
the bones will remain
to tell their own fragmentary tale.

The Chronic Cough

It isn't wise to try to suppress a cough—
the forceful, even violent aspirating effort—
a bronchial hacking reflex to extirpate
the sputum of frothy mucus. Sure,

the cough is an unwelcome neighbor
who has moved into the house,
insinuated himself ingratiatingly
into the daily routine—interrupting

every conversation with his incessant
complaint until you want to cry,
Stop, Stop, Please—knowing it's useless.
He won't listen to reason. Anyway he can't

control himself—it's his nature to take over
and demand an audience—he's an honorary member
of the bar who'd shout down Clarence Darrow.

This explains his rude behavior.
He is the child who can't be seen
but will be heard.

Hiccups

The origin of hiccup is hiccough as in
he coughed and coughed. When I lost
my file, I asked the technician what went wrong.
"The computer hiccuped," he said.
"How do it know?" my sister-in-law
Carol asks, but hiccups aren't just any glitch.
A hiccup is a periodic, spasmodic
closure of the glottis
resulting in a lowering
of the diaphragm. Try
jumping up and down,
being tickled, getting scared.
Take nine gulps of water
with your pinkie in your left ear.

In high school, when I asked
my best friend, Amy, to marry me,

she blinked,

the manifestation of a mental hiccup.

Maybe hiccups are built into the program,
like the fuzzy logic of chaos theory
or a pocket of low air pressure,
a sudden jerking-undertow,
a patch of sand on the bike path,
a sliver of black ice on the nighway.
You may crash. You may fall.
You may go under.
You need to go with the flow,
the Tao, the chi, the why
not?

Concussion

A concussion is never a coup de grâce
but a coup d'état. The head
remains in place though violently shaken.
The injury results from the blow to the skull or the end

of the spine—a ringing check to the boards
or a helmet to helmet collision in the open field—the brain
jangled from the high velocity impact
with an unforgiving object. Then transient dizziness

leads to loss of function, the inability
to remember one's name, or count fingers,
or follow simple directions, or walk without support.
In extreme cases shock results in seizures

and paralysis from cerebral lesions
that act like neurophysiological hiccups
or a chronic hacking cough that rocks the body with spasms
until the body cries, I give I give.

Clarity

is usually an illusion,
the water in the kettle pond
seems so clear—you can still see
your feet rooted in the sand
when you're standing up to your neck.
Yet you know it's full of life,
the detritus of fish, algae and pollen...
So we fool ourselves into thinking we know
the meaning of love, our reason
for being, what comes next,
because we sometimes seem to see clearly
as L. Ron Hubbard says we should.
He studied yoga, meditation, the mystery
of Eastern religions, and saw
opportunity. What if you meditated
not on no-thing, or on your own breath,
but on success? What if you focused
your energy on what you wanted?
Without doubt you would achieve
your heart's desire. All it takes
is knowing you're right.
All it takes is clarity.

Dark Matter

--90% of the universe is dark matter

It is what lies beneath
the surface of our lives.
We can't see it,
but we know it's there.
Like black holes,
it bends light.
It is what goes
unsaid.

It is the puddle
in the shadow at night—
it is the spirit of the dead,
friend, father, mother, lover,
one who visits you
in dreams.

It clouds the dreams
you can't quite recall,
the memories that remain
at the edge of your mind.

It is the phantom pain
of missing limbs.
It is the white worm
in America's soul.

Volcano Park

In case you forgot
what burns beneath,
pay a visit to Pele,
goddess of the volcano,
on the big island of Hawaii
where a fire-river of lava
tunnels through molten rock.
You can catch Kilauea's flow—
luminous at night—
from black pahoehoe cliffs
that overlook Kau loa Point.
Locals call it the witch's nose.
Gleaming lava cascades from her mouth
into the Pacific where it clashes
with crashing waves, crackles and spits
steam and gas into a vast sky.
Just in case you forgot what simmers
two miles beneath.

Shark Attack

Big waves call swimmers and surfers like sirens
while you scan the sea for signs of shark.
You seem to see them where they're not.
"There's one!" you say, pointing straight out.

"That's a seal!" your ten year old squeals.
"Right," you laugh and both dive in for a swim.
Still, you'll open your eyes underwater
where you are legally blind,

swear you can see the triple grin—rows of jagged teeth
beneath the sensitive nose—what sharks use to hunt
way beyond our range.

Know you'll react too late
to his claim for an arm or a leg,
a simple matter of mistaken identity,
human for seal. He could care less

about you. Hunger drives him
so close to shore
where you dare trespass
in his watery world.

Swimming

--the human body is 60-70% water

So we're floating,
sort of, not
sinking under water
but immersed
in water, wet
inside.
Not drowning,
swimming
in schools,
in cities,
and elsewhere,
happy or unhappy
as whales in pods
singing our songs,
circumnavigating
our world.

Field

Sure I get tired of being stepped on
but mostly I say, Go ahead friends,
take a seat why don't you
lie down and relax. Stare up
at the sky. Ignore
those moist patches
on the back of your pants.

Now try standing all together
with everyone you know
and everyone they know,
shoulder to shoulder,
arm in arm. Forget about going
anywhere. Instead wait
for the sun to surprise you
and the moon to remind you
of the passage of time.
Let the ants do their intricate work
while Robins fish for worms
and foxes fool rabbits.
Let the wind blow right through you.
Don't be afraid to bend and wave.

A Murder of Crows

Here, in the suburbs, crow gangs
line telephone wires
squawking, "what's up,"
drowning out finches, chickadees,
cardinals, mockingbirds.
If there's anything crows hate,
it's pretty birds with silly songs.

Crows respect friends who find road kill.
When a chipmunk's maimed by a passing car,
crows swoop down, cawing to every crow they know,
"party time!" After the feast
they strut the street like teamsters,
beaks curved cynically down,
wisecrack on the tip of the tongue.

If they had hands, they'd smoke blunts.
If they could talk, they'd call out bets,
"Ten bucks says the squirrel gets squished by a truck."
"Caw, caw, caw"—they laugh to beat the band.

Coyote in the Suburbs

1.

Coyote stalks stealthily on his toes,
ears point up, bushy tail sticks
straight back before he attacks.
At night his lonely howl
calls females to join,
warns males, "stay away,"
in case he missed a spot
marking his newly acquired territory.
Coyote links dog and wolf,
likes neither, roams in packs
or alone as long as food abounds.

Today food abounds in the burbs, baby.
Coyote catches bunnies by surprise,
calls mice a nice snack, stray cats
a tasty treat, and puppies,
yummy! He kinda likes it here,
quiet tree-lined streets,
undeveloped wetlands,
occasional woods. True,
no chickens, no sheep, no crisp
mountain-springs. Then again,
no ranchers with guns.
No open season year round.

2.

Barrel tipped over, lid off, trash bags ravaged,
remnants of corn, beans and hot dogs
trailing out to the street. At first I thought
it had to be the work of crows,
a skunk, perhaps an opossum,
until I heard late at night
the long plaintive howls.

Then my two-year-old and I spotted the coyote
one August evening
as we played on the deck after dinner.

He was stalking Angel, the neighbor's cat.
We saw his tail rise and his ears point
as he padded soundlessly behind the hedge.
Back turned, Angel licked her paws and purred.
Coyote bolted out of the bushes
and caught her in his jaws
before she could skedaddle.
She whined and scratched as he carried her off.
He grinned ear to ear. Oh yes,
a fat cat will make a fine meal—
Better keep the toddler on the deck after dusk.

Vampire Bat

Wedge-shaped incisor teeth
slash the skin of your victims.
You feed on their blood—
saliva makes it flow like wine.

In exchange, you offer rabies,
a fatal virus attacking the nervous system
like an army of viral ants.

Meanwhile you return to your cave.
Sated, you hang upside down
to sleep and dream,
like the rest of us, of breeding.

Killdeer at Stonehill

In June, robins hunt field mice in the quad.
A mockingbird fools a cardinal into thinking
he has friends in the area. I see a killdeer,
farm bird returning to the site of a former farm,
resting under a maple. I creep up
to get a better look, expecting she'll take off,
yet she remains and begins cheeping in protest—
"Deeyee," she says, "deeyee." I see
the fear and anger in her eyes,
and spot the four grey-speckled eggs
in the nest behind her.

Suddenly I remember driving along old 6A on Cape Cod.
The car in front stopped short.
I swerved around to his left,
hitting my brakes too late when I saw
the mother and six ducklings
waddling single-file across the road.

"I won't harm your eggs," I tell the killdeer, backing off.
"They're safe," I tell her, "for now."

Winter Fog in Boston

In winter the fog rises out of the earth
like the dead whose gray Puritan garb
disguises their every move. Still
you feel their pain in your bones.

You shiver and hug yourself for warmth.
Your teeth chatter—this is the language
they understand and fog
is the land they inhabit.

Their shadows follow you home
where they sing you to sleep
because you love them still.

The Elm

--for Emily

The elm remains green and keeps
His leaves late into the fall
despite Wind's warning,
"Winter's on the way." He stands tall
and lonely on our street,
lost amid the maple, birch and pine.
He doesn't seem to mind the wait;
there's time enough to die
and be reborn in Spring—a fate
we would happily emulate
if not for the unfortunate
finality of Death.

Hot Enough

There are days I wake up sick to death
of the taste of life which sticks
to my teeth like pitch. And when I look

through the closed finger-printed windows
I see nothing but gray, a massive front
that hovers over the houses, laden with moisture,

humid, mote-filled air that clots my lungs.
I can barely breathe in this heat and pray
for the rain that falls, if it falls at all, in globs

that muddle the dust-covered streets.
Showers offer little relief from the heat
which yawns on heedlessly,

mindlessly august in its languid reign.
I'll remain in bed as long as I can wallow
like a sow in the sweat-soaked sheets.

I'd rut in heat with my lover who sleeps nude beside me
but I can't bear to touch another, hate the thought
of the sight of my own fat self. Anyway

I have nothing of worth to say to her.
My tongue is covered with wool.
My mouth dry as rust.

If I could reach the razor, I'd draw
it like a string across my throat
but I can't even move.

The Moat around Your Heart

When breathing is an effort you just might
lie back down where you can float
in the moat around your heart.

Your breath labors to find
a rhythm you can bear
like the child you never had,

or the child you did have
but lost, or the child you lost track of.
At times like this it's hard to keep track
of the train of your thought

which follows the tracks on into the tunnel
and seems to go on forever.
Or maybe it's just tunnel vision.

If only you could get back
on track you might recover
a reason for being here,
or there, or anywhere at all.

At The Pool

On a languid afternoon in July,
we lounge by the condominium pool,
the octogenarian widows who occupy fold-out chairs,
gossiping and whining about the heat, the humidity,
the water temperature (too cold),
and the stay-at-home moms
with their shy boys, bossy girls.

I'm there with Eddie who's learning to swim,
paddling furiously to keep his head
above the water while I float
on my back, happily buoyant,
as if I am blown up with air. I drift

aimlessly, the sun so bright I can see it
with my eyes closed. Swimming
in the water, hands weaving like fins,
feet flapping like flukes,
I dive under—it is so quiet,
my ears nearly close
and turn into gills.

The End of Summer

You can hardly blame August for the slow
heat that has your molecules dancing.

August hangs onto summer
like an old lover. The days
stretch out like hands
reaching across the bed.

The sun, unyielding at noon,
seems ready to take the plunge
into the ocean after dinner.
He singes the sky orange as he sinks.

Still, isn't it always dark
sooner than you expect?

Driving Montana in August

Out here the haze shimmers off the road in the heat.
In the distance shapes shift and dance—
could be stray cows or coyotes
or even mountain lions on the prowl.

You slow down to make sure
your mind isn't engendering images,
like this, out of thin air.

Not here, where
the air is far from thin,
but pregnant with possibilities,
fraught with the meaning you ascribe
as you drive into the sun.

The Flying Dutchman

When the barometer drops you feel the pressure
on your frontal lobe. Your forehead rolls forward
and your brow pulls you down like a yoke

as you drag the plow behind, one foot
in front of the other. And if it weren't
so dry and dusty, you might be

underwater, laboring like Hercules
for breath. You might be lost at sea
like the Flying Dutchman—

there was something you had to do,
someone you had to find,
a port in which to anchor,

land to claim, seed to sow...
You forget what, yet you push on
out of habit or necessity, mopping sweat,

swatting flies, grumpy and unsatisfied—
meanwhile papers pile up on your desk;
the e-mail file is full; your muted cell phone
vibrates in your pocket...

Dear Mr. Frost

I've been meaning to write for advice.
I realize it's a little late—delight,
I understand. It's how you get
from there to wisdom that puzzles me.
Naturally, I want to be whole again,
beyond confusion, and so I drink.
But I remain confused,
as if I'd wandered
onto the road not taken
and gotten lost.
Not that that makes any difference.
Now I'm on the fence
about what to do next.
Return to earth I suppose—
earth's the right place for love,
though "it's a good fence,"
my neighbor claims. In any case,
as I was asking before Truth stepped in,
any tips, Mr. Frost,
for once then, something?

Connie

"Earthe Toc of Erthe"
(Anonymous ca 1000, UK)

You pulled your boots back on and drew
your thin legs up, jeans on the floor,
flannel shirt unbuttoned, long dirty-
blond hair hiding the sharp bones
of your shoulders. You propped
yourself up on elbows and kept

Earthe toc of erthe erthe wyth woh,

your eyes open, waiting for me to finish.
You were not a good fuck, Connie.
Yet we had all fucked you—Jimmy,
Vinny, Murph and me, because

erthe other erthe to the erthe droh,

you made yourself available.
Jimmy fucked you weekly,
the others once or twice.
That one time I was there
(as one of the guys). You had no
girlfriends. You hung out with us.

erthe leyde erthe in erthene throh

We gave you grass, downs, a couch to crash on,
until one morning, senior year,
Jimmy woke up hung over
and tossed your boots out on the lawn—

tho hevede erthe of erthe erthe ynoh.

just like that, you were gone.
It was a big campus, UMass,
20,000 kids. You could fuck someone
and never see them again.

At The Wake

I'm wondering, Mark, how many you gave
the back of your hand
whenever they asked for it.
"They got what they wanted," you said.
"Some of us like it a little rough,"
Paula once said to me, smiling, drunk,
skirt hiked up in the back seat
of my Charger RT. We were all
on Tequila and downs, going two ways
at once. She still had the black eye
she got from you. I fucked her harder,
her nails in the back of my neck,
her teeth in my lower lip.
She sucked my blood but when she came
she called your name, Mark.

Twenty years later she downed
a script of Percocet at home
after her shift at the club.
At the wake her corpse looked good,
hair dyed black, violet eyes shut.
"She's better off dead," her sister Carla said.
You nodded to me across the room.
I thought of the one time we'd fought—
my left crossing over your right—
we both went down. "Stay away
from Paula," you said. I laughed
and spit blood, but I did
stay away, while you went back
and took all she had to give.

Family Photo

My wife wants me to remove
the furrow in my brow
for the family photo.

I am already smiling,
        doing my best
to look happy.

I raise my eyebrows
knowing the vacant look
that will result,

as if I'd been caught
in a white lie
about the drink I snuck
moments ago.

My face drops
as the shutter clicks.
You can just guess
how it turns out.

Song of Suicide

1.

Isn't suicide selfish? The act
of a narcissistic, self-indulgent adolescent
who can't see past his own shadow
and wallows in self-pity?
You could take the plunge
like Kurt Cobain
who failed to find
solace in Skag
and was addicted to depression
which comes over you in waves
till you want to wail
when Jack Daniels on the rocks
doesn't bring you down enough,
and heroin won't take you far enough,
unless you fill the needle
with the DNA of death
and take the plunge
into the cold depths,
or stare into the barrel of a shotgun,
thumb on the trigger,
but let's not go there—
it's depressing and I'm indulging
in self-pity when there are plenty
of other good reasons
to take yourself out.
Say you can't write another song—
it all sounds the same,
the whine of flat notes a monotone
that lulls you to sleep.
"Death's second self," Shakespeare wrote.
And "we're better off without you," you say,
thinking of Courtney whose career took off
after you checked out.
She isn't in your shadow anymore.
So the choice you made
worked out for her
and you knew we'd feel your pain

because suicides leave a black hole
where a person once was.
And those who visit your grave
feel drawn to your despair
because it's crazy to take your own life,
the life God gave you.
Smirking the cynical sneer of suicide, you ask,
"The same God who gave us AIDs?"

2.

Well if it's cowardly to kill yourself,
is it brave to remain unhappily alive?
Isn't it better to slit your wrists?
Put us all out of your misery?
Put a gun to your temple?
Turn the car on in the garage?
Jump. Jump. Go ahead and jump
from the Brooklyn Bridge, the Empire State, a cliff...
In Japan, suicide's an honorable option
if the shame is too great to live down.
Though disemboweling seems a bit atavistic.
It would be more Western to jump in the car,
take it out on a lonely road
in the wee hours of the night
before the pink rose of dawn blooms anew.
We'd cut the lights like James Dean,
wind blowing through our hair,
or Grace Kelly, lovely in her white scarf,
sunglasses filled with darkness,
or Antoine de Saint-Exupéry,
in search of another kingdom,
or Camus, estranged from himself.
Here in America, we'd be drunk,
swerving across the white lines,
finding it hard to focus,
no idea where we're going,
the darkness a wall we all want to drive though.

Jessica Follows Her Dream

--Jessica Dubroff, 1989-1996

Little Jessica always wanted to "fly high in the sky." Jessica's mom and dad only wanted what was "best for their little girl." Jessica had a dream to be the youngest girl ever to fly across America, to sit at the controls, hands on the wheel, eyes on the clouds, the altimeter, the gas gauge, the air pressure, the compass, keeping the nose up, wings stable, keeping contact via headphones with her dad who would be right there behind her in another plane for safety's sake while her mom would be waiting down below for her little girl to follow her dream, as all of us should, here in America.

And that's the story—a real corker Murphy Brown might say—little poster fly-girl-Jessica follows her dream and lifts her parents out of debt to follow their dream, make the front page, write the book, hit the talk-show circuit, pitch the movie to Paramount insisting on a percentage of the gross at the gate. Jessica's mom may still achieve that dream, although the story has changed from heroic to tragic, it still sounds made for TV.

It's unfortunate, of course, Jessica and her dad had to die. Everyone feels just terrible. Her mom most of all, not to mention the reporters and photographers who were invested, many of them emotionally, which was really why they got into journalism in the first place. Hey you don't come across a story like that every day. Careers are made on such stories, and now little Jessica lives on in our memories, along with the images and stories of all of those who have died on TV, in the newspapers, on the radio, in the magazines.

The Prompt

The prompt is the color blue picked out of a hat,
and someone in a raincoat with a reason for being there.
Elements of a short story or a novel or maybe
a narrative poem employing Keat's negative capability...

Say you put yourself beneath a blue sky on your way
to meet someone. You wear your raincoat
because Emily, the ditzy weathergirl, cheerily predicted rain.
Now you feel betrayed by her, the weather,
and the government. Meanwhile, the sun
burns your eyes, sunglasses left home.
You grip an umbrella like a weapon
until your hand turns blue waiting for the light to change.
Turns out you're negative but incapable
of crossing the street—never mind
assuming a persona.

Yet we all assume a persona
whenever we don the raincoat
we don't necessarily need
in case it rains while we're waiting
for someone or something to change
our ignominious lives.

Frost Country

From Breadloaf, I jog downhill towards town.
I pass Wayside, site of the cabin where Frost
spent summers writing poems. It's a stone's throw
from the Frost House on Frost Road. There,
a yellow bus unloads middle school kids.
I imagine the clouds shape the old poet's craggy head,
cusp of a smile on his puffy face. Then I see a sign
for the Frost Interpretive Trail. I weave
through the parking lot past a Camry
and a mini-van. On the trail poems on plaques
intersperse with verses carved in wood.
Caught between delight and wisdom, I hesitate
at the fork for "The Road Not Taken."
Then I realize, it's a loop!
It doesn't make any difference
which path you choose. You end up
back in the parking lot
with the Camry and the min-van.

At the Lake in Maine

While loons croon
their mellifluous lullaby

beneath the beguiling susurrations
of innumerable stars,

fireflies flicker
in the overgrown garden,

illuminating the ethereal insouciance
of the angels

who fall silently
in our midst
like diaphanous dreams.

The Word-Present

"*Rhinoceros, now that's a one-word poem.*"
(Robert Bly)

1.

Her sister Sarah gave her a word-present for Christmas
and now she was unwrapping it for us
in a wedding toast. She was the Maid of Honor,
the successful older sister.
She admitted she'd worked too much
and lost her husband, ate too much
and lost her figure. Now
she was rebalancing the scales
because she wanted what her sister Sarah had.
And she wanted to be able
to give her a word-present.

And the word—balance—
with equal weight on both sides
and the "l" stretched like a tightrope
in between, exactly
what she lacked in her life.
Yet she returned the gift unused.
Though she sorely needed it,
she didn't like hearing it
from her younger sister.
And now I'm giving it, with love,
to you, friends.
        —balance—

2.

But isn't it presumptuous
to give someone a word
as a present? Doesn't it assume
that you know what the person needs
or wants or deserves

and that it is embodied in a word
that the recipient is somehow

58

unaware of
yet will benefit from,
see the import of,
and take to heart?

Is it a word poem, then?
Are poems presents,
boxes of words
wrapped in books?

Under the Full Moon

"...the original date rape drug."
(Brenda Shaughnessy)

What kind of lunacy is that Brenda?
Have I been sleepwalking through life
while your menstrual cycle
synched with Silene's, the Titan goddess,
the girl of my dreams,
her chariot drawn by winged steeds,
the original Valkyrie,
my very own Siren
calling me out to fly
across the seas,
beyond Tranquility,
a giant leap for this mankind.
Still you can run with me any night.
We both know who to blame
for the change that morphs us all
when the moon blooms with light.

Anxiety

shakes you awake,
undermining your resolve
to sleep though the night.
The feeling of fright,
palpable as sweat,

the bet you had with yourself
lost...the cost of your self-esteem
or what's left of it.

The hairs on the back of your neck
erect. Tell yourself
you'll get through this,
the lie you'll need to believe.

Elbow

1.

You can be pushy,
insinuating yourself
into a group
to interrupt the conversation,
or when slicing through the crowd
for a drink at the bar,
or wending and weaving
to the stage
so I can imbibe to the band.

You can be swung like an ax
among the trees,
beneath the boards in basketball,
sharp enough to split skin and crack ribs.

I like to lean on you
when I'm trying to think
of what to write,
although it's impolite
at the dinner table
to put too much weight on you.
You can be funny
when you strike a nerve
and send a frisson
of temporary paralysis
buzzing through the bone.

Mostly you're a hinge,
hanging out—friend
to the hand. You help
get work done.

2.

Maybe it was you who
prevented poetry
from being pushed out altogether
because back in the day
poetry was the entire body
of work—the whole kit
and caboodle. But slowly,
century by century our goddess
was dismembered—
first to go was history,
followed by mythology,
and all that drama.
She lost her form, her rhythm,
until there was little left
but lyric and confession.
Then surprisingly, recently
poetry took an imaginary leap,
up off the mat,
fighting back in rap
and song and spoken word,
reclaiming form and substance,
to claw and elbow her way back
onto the stage.

Who to Blame

When I fractured my knee
I became one of the lame.
You see us on the streets,
moving slow as peat, faces
grimacing.

I can't explain
exactly how it feels
to be a useless fuck,
dependent on the State

or someone you love.
It sucks all right.
Although it's good to know
it will eventually end—

unlike the plight of those
disabled for life,
feet blown off by terrorists,
or rocked by IEDs in Iraq,
or "friendly fire" in Afghanistan,

or maybe a misguided drone.
Sometimes you have to wonder
who the enemy really is.
I wonder who to blame
as I limp my way home.

Crutches

--For Betsy

Eventually you'll probably need them,
wooden or aluminum, either way,
something you can lean on.
They come in pairs, like swans
that fit snugly under your arms,
right up to the pits.
Though it's your arms
you have to use
to keep the weight
off the broken ankle, fractured
knee, torn ligaments, displaced
tibial plateau, but what I meant
was how marriage can be a crutch
you lean on when things go wrong,
an injury, illness, loss of work, a fall
off the wagon, an arrest—
It's always never your fault.
So it's good to have someone
willing, on occasion, to stand mute,
feathers unruffled, a mate for life.

America

Regret is an overcoat
you don daily
no matter what
the weather is.
You don't get to leave
your fugly memories
behind. Maybe that's why
you indulge in self-pity.
Don't the people you hurt
deserve some pain
for making the fatal mistake
of loving you?
You can't claim
to ever be free
of blame. It is your fault,
after all, and that's
the seismic shift
that unsettles your soul
and may at any moment
quake your world.

1969

We thought we could do anything we wanted:
popping hallucinogens, envisioning life
a pinball game we saw ourselves winning,
bouncing from one girl or boy to another,
waiting for that KNOCK

that meant we'd won again—
can you blame us? The flashing lights,
the bells and whistles, sex
with beautiful people we hardly knew—

the silver balls seemed endless,
lined up and ready to go, and the music,
our very own rock, sounded even better high.

We were drunk on our own Kool-Aid—
electric wine passed around with joints.
So in love with who we thought we were,
we imagined our utopian dreams real.

Talk About Luck

Tommy gunned his Chevy SS,
smoking rubber, squealing tires,
what passed for cool at our high school
as we left the graduation party behind,
buzzed on Buds, tossing empties
at the cheerleaders on the lawn,
the local cops filled our rearview,
turned on the bubblegum
and strafed the air with sirens.

Richard riding gun, me in back,
Tommy took Brush Hill way up
past the reservoir and lost the cops for good
when he cut through the cemetery.

On Gunhill, he floored it just for fun.
At the rotary we felt the tires lose their grip.
We hit the stone wall dead on at 60.
It didn't give much. We all crawled
out the driver's side window,
shaking glass from our hair.
Tommy's ribs were cracked, my ankle broken,
Richard's face bloodied from the fissure
that divided his forehead.
We couldn't think straight or stand up.
It was a Sunday—the roads eerily empty.
Another kid, Dick Church, found us
and ferried us to the hospital in his VW van.
Talk about luck.

Doctor Wilson

Doctor Wilson runs a health clinic in Madison. Ten years ago, he lived next door with big Marge, little Aaron, and Jarrett. Marge had two addictions: the Shopping Channel and Snickers Bars. One Saturday we helped her cut up credit cards. "Prozac anyone? Diet pills?" asked Doctor Wilson. The boys, 6 and 8 years old, were downstairs watching *Nightmare on Elm Street*. "They love horror flicks," Marge said.

We thought Marge and Peter whacked the boys around, though we couldn't be sure. We'd hear Marge say, "Get in here you little shit. Clean up this fucking mess." We figured Jarrett was acting out when he beat up Aaron or knocked our son down with a stone the size of a softball.

Aaron seldom spoke and hummed unnamed tunes to himself while torturing dolls in the driveway. Weekends, they'd all go out and leave their collie, Elvis, chained to the house where he'd bark himself horse. Still, I was surprised when Doctor Wilson rang my bell one afternoon to complain that my son had used profane language. "He called Jarrett a shithead," he said, clenching and unclenching his hands, wet with sweat.

"You're the shithead," I said and slammed the door. Later I heard the Doctor shooting his rifle in his back yard. I watched out the window as he showed his kids how. He told them: aim at the trees, not at the birds.

One weekend in August, they cleared out. They'd declared bankruptcy. The bank sold the house. They moved to Wisconsin where Doctor Wilson had been hired to run a health clinic.

Mall Story

We sat and waited
wondering why
we were there. Then
you appeared wearing
your big sister's Uggs,
smug and unyielding.
We'd follow you anywhere.
This was before the drugs
took hold and seized control
of your soul
and turned it black
with hate. And before
we knew it, too late
for you. So
we moved on,
left you behind.
We use you now
to remind us
what not to do.

After the Wake

Like ink smeared on paper,
gray clouds tarred the sky.
You were quarantined by grief,

refracted by time. You didn't mind
the heavy rain, the pain
gone underground, underneath

the grief, despair.
The only trace: the grimace
on your face.

Ghosts

The end of the year is near.
The day is a gray cat—she scampers across
the cold hard grass. The light

steals over the field like a ghost.
Night is the cat's long shadow.
Though we flood the darkness with light,

the night remains peopled
with all our fears, all our failures.
Darkness follows the day home.

What You Know

After being comfortable,
decide enjoyment feels good,
having income—justified;

know love makes necessary
overall perfection.
Quietly remember sorrow.

Tomorrow understand,
value wildness.
X-chromosome your zen.

What the Body Knows

Wasn't Michael Jordan a genius of hang-gliding, tongue wagging
dunks?
Not to mention 15 foot jumpers, 12 foot leaners, reverse finger rolls.
Wasn't the brilliance of Larry Bird the no-look,
behind the neck pass beneath the boards?
Or was it the in-your-face 3-pointer
with time running out?

Maybe it's an art—Big Pappi's swing
baseball ballet. The over the shoulder catch
by Willy Mays at a dead run in center field,
or a back-handed stab by Nomar Garciapara,
deep in the hole, and a side-arm throw
across his outstretched body to nail the runner at first—
expressions of a body of wisdom to our delight.

Wasn't there a game when you too saw the basket
with startling clarity just as you released the ball
knowing it all net? Or a time when the baseball
hung in the air like the Miami sun and the bat—
an eclipse waiting to happen?

Haven't we all had one game when we couldn't miss?
As if the body suddenly remembered
what it could do if it wanted to.
We had somehow stumbled into the zone
of great athletes. We were somewhere between
mind and body, in a land of deep focus
where the voices without and the voices within were fans
and the game in all its antediluvian glory--all there was.

More or Less

Less is more I guess; it's best
not to dwell on what's left
undone, or run away
from all that we suppress—
the Presidents that we elect,
the evidence that we ignore:
take the poor in New Orleans
who happen to be black, unseen.
But, you say, we don't mean
to be mean. Or take Iraq--
we merely meant
to replace Saddam
And secure the peace, not the oil!
Whose fault is it when they fail
to create a democratic state?
Now we wait for someone else
To seize control, direct our fate.

Giant Penguins

For three months the sun shines,
the ice melts and the Giant Penguins
dive from the banks into the bracing water,
filling their bellies with fish,

basking in the endless sun;
they grow fat without worry.
But soon the days grow short--the earth
turns away from the sun

and the penguins gather on the shore--
all dressed up and nowhere to go--
they huddle, their young on their feet,
feeding beak to beak. In the howling snow

and bitter wind, they grow lean with hunger.
In the dead of winter they have only each other.
If they had wings, they would fly south,
but all they can do is stand and wait.

White Crest Beach

Grains of sand tangle our hair
as the ocean advances
up the beach behind our backs
and water invades the inlets

between our toes. I roll over
onto my back
and you kiss the salt
off my lips, your head looming above

eclipses the sun; your blond hair
shades my face. I see your mouth curl:
pearl necklace on display.

When you pull away, shafts of light
shutter my eyes and my skin
offers the annual cellular sacrifice:
small price for this bliss.

What I'll Miss

Swimming with you in a glacial pond in Wellfleet
--water warmer than air in September—
so clear you can see twenty feet down,
perch flitting in between—miniature
submarines. It takes us all summer
to get to where we can swim
across and back Dyer Pond.

We relearn to relax and breathe,
turning heads to capture air,
returning to a fluid world
our bodies seem to remember
somewhere beyond thought—our arms extend
to pull and push the water behind
where legs scissor and feet paddle.
We slice through--smooth as seals.

Maybe this is the world we'll return to—
the one we were baptized in,
the one we spent most of our first year,
hooked up, enveloped, floating
in viscous warmth
until we grew too big to carry
and had to emerge
into the light of this world.

Could it be like that? Not heaven
but the murky dusk of our subconscious
where now we nightly float
and where we will return to remember
how to breathe and swim and see.